THE RICH RULE OVER ....

THE BORROWER IS A SLAVE TO THE LENDER.

FAITHFUL
ABUNDANCE

JEAN LOUIS HARDY

"What is to give light must endure burning"
Viktor Frankl

Unless God is that fire and light, then you will be untouched...
Exodus 3:2-5

The book is written in such a way that you should have a bible to check the verses, it's best if you have a bible and read the verses more than once, this will plant the seed of God's word deep in your heart.

Be blessed, and may God's face shine on you.

TABLE OF CONTENTS

INTRO

This is a personal story about how I came to the conclusion of some of the principles you will learn in the book, let's dive in!

Proverbs 22:7

The rich rule over the poor, and the borrower is a slave to the lender."

There was a time when, in my household, money was considered something sacred, yet still evil. It was a paradox wrapped in green paper—a symbol of both security and sin. Money's omnipresence shaped our existence, dictating our choices and casting long shadows over our daily lives. He who had the money, ruled over us. I didn't know it at the time, but looking back I see how real this verse is.

This dynamic is particularly challenging because, from the ages of 0 to 7, children are the most impressionable.

These formative years shape our understanding of the world and set the stage for how we live the rest of our lives. According to child development experts, early experiences significantly impact brain development, influencing cognitive, social, and emotional growth. The duality of wealth and morality during my childhood left an indelible mark on me. It created a complex landscape in my young mind, where money was both a blessing and a curse.

Now, picture this being thrust into the everyday world, where your potential as a child is both limitless and yet constrained by the environment it is born into. This was my reality. Money and who had it was the force that controlled our household, yet money was often whispered about with a strange reverence mixed with fear. It was both a blessing and a curse, a double-edged sword that shaped our lives.

As a child, I watched as whoever had the money dictated our choices and relationships. I saw my mother entangled with people who had wealth but lacked moral grounding, creating a confusing backdrop for my understanding of prosperity, yet she relied on them to make ends meet. It was a complex world where money seemed to offer freedom but also chained us with invisible bonds and certain relationships.

This duality of experiences set the stage for a long journey of grappling with these concepts and ultimately led to a profound spiritual awakening. It took years for me to realize that money, in itself, is neutral. It is merely a tool, and he who possesses the tool has the power to rule and make decisions.

Proverbs 22:7 says, "The rich rule over the poor, and the borrower is a slave to the lender." This verse became a beacon of truth, highlighting the power dynamics that money creates, it was clear it was a tool that gave the PERSON power, itself was not power.

The mission I embrace today is clear: to reveal the truth about God's promises, which are always "yes and Amen" (2 Corinthians 1:20), for everyone willing to listen. It's about breaking free from the deceptive beliefs that equate poverty with righteousness or that wealth automatically signifies closeness to God. Money is a tool, and God's abundance is limitless. There is something to say about having wealth and being a child of God, but more on that later in the book.

When you read Haggai 2:8: "The silver is mine, and the gold is mine, declares the Lord of hosts." Can you see how this verse highlights God's ultimate ownership of all material wealth, reinforcing His sovereignty? It also points to the fact that He has the authority to give or take away the power that comes with wealth! This is an important perspective to hold on to. God does not delight in seeing His people ruled by money or people who have it and are wicked. Whether it's through the false belief that poverty sanctifies us or the illusion that riches bring us closer to Him, or that we have to rely on a worldly source to support us, He wants to bless us abundantly through wisdom and work.

This blessing isn't found in wealth itself but in the freedom it affords us to deepen our relationship with Him and be creative in the world. This way, we can express more of His attributes and become more like Him. God wants us to enjoy the things he created, for the person who likes to travel he wants them to seek Him in that, for the person who loves food, He wants to share the experiences that it gives. These things are good.

It's almost like if we are Christians we are not to enjoy the good things that God has put on this earth. God just asks us to NOT make idols out of them.

Ephesians 2:10 tells us, "For we are God's handiwork, created in Christ Jesus to do good works, which God prepared in advance for us to do." When we use our freedom to express creativity and good works, while enjoying the fruits of our labor, we reflect His nature and fulfill His purpose for our lives. When we are wealthy, the only ruler we have over us is God. That is a massive responsibility, that's quite a bit of freedom. God is all about freedom, God wants to share that freedom with us since he owns all wealth.

1 John 3:17 emphasizes this principle: "If anyone has material possessions and sees a brother or sister in need but has no pity on them, how can the love of God be in that person?"

Let us be open to being financially free to glorify God.

This book is a small journey to understand how aligning our financial pursuits with divine principles unlocks true prosperity. It's not about the figures in your bank account but about the time and freedom to seek God more earnestly. Together, we will explore the sacred balance between wealth and spirituality, discovering that true prosperity is not just about having more but about being more—more generous, more faithful, and more aligned with God's divine will.

CHAPTER 1:
UNCOVERING THE LIE

"Money isn't the most important thing in life, but it's reasonably close to oxygen on the 'gotta have it' scale."
— Zig Ziglar

Imagine, if you will, a single utterance—softly spoken, perhaps in a very important conversation about how to lead your life — this one utterance, this one word will produce two stark realities: one of boundless joy, the other a relentless gloom. Wouldn't you listen intently and hear every syllable?

What if "Money is the root of all evil..." was said to you...?

What kind of life do you think that would produce? If you thought of poverty and relentless gloom when it comes to your finances, you guessed right. Most people who struggle with building wealth think to some degree that money is evil in some way shape or form.

This phrase is often used both jokingly and seriously, but what kind of trouble has it actually caused?

Scripture says to us in 1 Timothy 6:10, "For the love of money is a root of all kinds of evil." Ah, therein lies an overwhelming difference! Therein we can find the LIE that was fed to you on a silver spoon over and over...

The missing verse, "The Love of Money"

We could add "The Love of _____" or any idol is the root of all evil (except God, everything you like should seem as hatred comparatively Luke 14:26 "If anyone comes to me and does not hate father and mother, wife and children, brothers and sisters—yes, even their own life—such a person cannot be my disciple.)

It is the love, YES THE LOVE, the unrestrained worship of currency, that leads to the undoing of souls. It's not the money itself, the money has no power in itself other than to testify of what you have done with it.

Money itself is as morally neutral as a humble toaster. It toasts without judgment or passion, indifferent to your race, gender, background, or intelligence. If money had a desire, it would simply be to facilitate exchanges, content in its role once traded for another service or product.

Growing up around gang members and people who had money, I learned later that it wasn't the money that bred corruption. It was the pursuit of power and perceived freedom, and the unethical ways they dealt with others to obtain it. Their beliefs about money entangled them in a web of misguided actions.

Your actions regarding money reflect your beliefs, and your beliefs shape money's primary purpose in your life.

Smart does not equal money
Being good does not equal money
Being bad does not equals money
Being neutral to money and seeing it as a tool will allow you to do what you need to with proper guidance.

This now begs the question: What's the purpose of money?

I've observed with the curiosity of a cat watching a laser dot, those who vilify wealth and money as if it were the apple in Eden. They look upon the affluent with green eyes, not with wealth but with envy, assuming dark deeds paved the roads to riches. It's not always the case! In fact, most of the time, it's not the case at all. The rich see this neutral tool as an income-producing asset. its purpose is in the eye of the beholder.

The poor, who secretly desire wealth, are full of envy and constantly say things like, "Oh, wouldn't that be nice to have..." (Insert anything they just saw). Yet, they spurn anyone who has it as they would a leper—how can one embrace what one despises? Therefore, they will never be rich with that kind of attitude. Their belief about money is all wrong. They wear poverty as a badge of honor, as if some heavenly favor shone upon the destitute and the poor.

Remember, God said, "Blessed are the **poor in spirit**, for theirs is the kingdom of heaven" (Matthew 5:3), not those in material poverty. Here's a note: You cannot receive what you demonize. Misguided souls! They slumber in want, clutching the belief that scarcity is some divine decree, judge others for having more, yet never achieve their true purpose. While the rich are looking for a place to turn their $100 into $1,000.

I've observed that this type of thinking is the fastest way to poverty. If you have judged someone for being rich, it's time to ask God for forgiveness and look deep inside yourself to see why you would cast such stones. Think through this conundrum: you judge the rich, but when you go to church and your brother is blessed with a promotion, you praise God.

Don't you find this odd and hypocritical? We need to align money's purpose with God's and ours.

To embrace wealth, you must first correct your beliefs about money. It is not inherently good or evil; it is a tool. Your mindset shapes how you use it and whether you can attract it. Change your perspective, and you change your reality.

God's desire was not for us to be a broken people who had to scrape by financially and say "NO LORD" when a need came up for our brothers and sisters or even ourselves. 1 John 3:17

This symphony of sorrows, this parade of penury, all stem from a singular, serrated lie.

'Tis not money but its idolization that opens doors to the unpleasant danger of greed and malice—and herein lies the rub, the revelation that shakes the very foundation of any pauper's moral high ground.

For as you stand in the market square, pointing fingers at the rich, casting stones at their fortresses, speaking about their possessions and tyranny, you unwittingly wear the same cloak of evil that you cast the stone at. To decry wealth while elevating oneself for the lack thereof is to enter in the same murky waters of judgment and conceit.

Here's the unvarnished truth: in criticizing others for their wealth, you position yourself as the arbiter of righteousness, simply by virtue of your lack. meaning you subconsciously program the idea that being poor is good and rich is evil.

Hopefully this seems foolish now, with the information that the rich are just able to turn 1$ into 10$ because they made it a goal to look at money as a place to store assets, you now judge them?

Yet, this scale of virtue and vice is not weighted in gold but in intention. For the pauper can harbor a heart blackened by envy just as the prince can wield his wealth with benevolence.

God gave us a choice.
wait....
Can you hear that?

It's probably your conscious speaking saying "But how did the rich person get the money? they must have done something evil!" that's the proof of the programing.

Here's a proverb for your soul: *The blessing of the LORD makes one rich, And He adds no sorrow with it. Proverbs 10:22*

So, before we cast aspersions on the gilded halls and those who walk them, let us examine the mirrors of our souls.

Are we any less covetous, any more righteous? Perhaps, it is time to dismantle the pedestals we build from our own insufficiencies, recognizing that virtue is not measured by the weight of one's purse but by the weight of one's character.

God had to teach me this early. I used to see young kids driving in supercars and scoff " Phhh, daddy's money." When I would love it if my children did not have to endure poverty as I did when I was their age.

This double standard is the lie we are led to believe is acceptable. We should be grateful and thankful that someone left a good inheritance for their children.

Proverbs 13:22 A good man leaveth an inheritance to his children's children: and the wealth of the sinner is laid up for the just.

You see it's the worship of money that allows the spirits that tempt men to thievery, to the taking of bribes, to the infliction of pain for a fistful of fleeting treasures. and looking down on the rich, its envy that causes men to become stuck in poverty and not find their calling while they lie the wallows of sin.

When one dances with money, not as a master, but as God intended,to use it a tool and grow it for its purpose, it transforms. It becomes a steward of our growth, a tool to sculpt God's desires through us to others.

Letting Go of Self-Judgment and
Embracing True Prosperity

Find a quiet, comfortable place where you won't be disturbed. Close your eyes and take a few deep breaths, allowing your mind to calm, so we can focus.

Reflect on any beliefs you hold that associate poverty with righteousness. Recognize any thoughts that come to mind, such as "Being poor makes me more humble," or "God prefers those who have less." Notice the emotions these beliefs evoke in you, whether it's guilt, pride, or a sense of moral superiority.

Ask God if these beliefs truly align with God's word. How do they limit you or others? Reflect on 1 Timothy 6:17: "Command those who are rich in this present world not to be arrogant nor to put their hope in wealth, which is so uncertain, but to put their hope in God, who richly provides us with everything for our enjoyment." Understanding that God's provision comes from rich people, includes enjoying His blessings, not idolizing poverty.

Speak out loud: "I release the belief that poverty is righteous. I embrace the freedom and blessings that God intends for me."

Write down affirmations that reflect a balanced and healthy view of prosperity. Speak these affirmations out loud: "God desires for me to live abundantly and use His blessings for good."

"I can honor God through wise stewardship of the resources He provides."

"True righteousness comes from my relationship with God, not a financial status."

Pray for forgiveness for any thoughts or words spoken of guilt or superiority you have held regarding poverty and wealth. Say aloud: "I forgive myself for judging others for their wealth. I release any judgment I have held against them. We are all stewards of God's blessings."

Lets Pray: Heavenly Father, I come before You with a humble heart. I release the false belief that poverty is a sign of righteousness. Help me to see myself and others through Your eyes, free from judgment and envy. Teach me to embrace Your blessings with gratitude and use them to reflect Your love and generosity. In Jesus' name, Amen.

Each day, speak out loud three things you are grateful for. This practice shifts your focus from lack to abundance and helps reinforce a positive mindset.

By regularly practicing this mental exercise, you will learn to let go of self-judgment and the belief that poverty is inherently righteous. This shift in mindset will naturally reduce your tendency to judge others, fostering a healthier, more compassionate perspective on wealth and prosperity allowing God's blessing to flow where you'd want it too.

Jeremiah 29:11:
"For I know the plans I have for you," declares the LORD, "plans to prosper you and not to harm you, plans to give you hope and a future."

Sealed in the blood of Jesus, In Jesus name Amen.

CHAPTER 2:

MONEY'S CHARACTER

Proverbs 11:24-25: "One person gives freely, yet gains even more; another withholds unduly, but comes to poverty. A generous person will prosper; whoever refreshes others will be refreshed."

Money, since the beginning of its conception, has played a pivotal role; we know this due to how much the bible talks about it. Though it may be just a tool; It has one human characteristic that we cannot ignore.

Money has a voice.

With its voice it echoes in both earthly and spiritual realms. This may sound like a whimsical notion, but it's deeply rooted in biblical wisdom that shows how our financial decisions extend far beyond the physical world.

Let's begin with the paradox laid out in Proverbs 11:24-25.

It presents a counterintuitive principle: generosity leads to gain, while withholding leads to poverty.

This goes against the common belief that accumulating wealth is the key to security.

However, the Bible reveals a deeper spiritual reality where true prosperity is rooted in generosity—a concept that operates on a spiritual plane intersecting with our daily lives. Things like being honest and generous with your employees, giving a fair wage and understanding their value.

About money's voice..

Consider James 5:4: "Behold, the wages of the laborers who mowed your fields, which you kept back by fraud, are crying out against you, and the cries of the harvesters have reached the ears of the Lord of hosts."

Here, we see that the wages unjustly withheld have their own voice!

A testimony against those who engage in fraud. This isn't mere poetry; it's a spiritual truth. Money mishandled or unjustly withheld carries a testimony, a witness against its handler. It's a stark reminder that how we deal with money is significant to God, and it will either commend or condemn us in the spiritual realm.

Just to seal the point in your heart, those who are rich, yet deal unjustly, that money will become a witness against you!

James 5:3 Your gold and silver are corroded, and their corrosion will be a witness against you and will eat your flesh like fire. You have heaped up treasure in the last days

In other words their money will become molten lava and burn them forever.

Needless to say, you don't want to be this type of person.

Money's dual nature as a potential blessing or curse is evident. It can promote us or expose us, depending on our stewardship. You might argue, "But what about those seemingly unscrupulous rich individuals who prosper without a care for these principles?"

True, their success might seem unaffected by these principles for now.

Yet, as children of God, are we not held to a higher standard? accountable not just to earthly laws but to divine principles?

Money, then, becomes a witness. It speaks to the integrity—or lack thereof—of its possessor. In the spiritual realm, every dollar and cent testifies to our character and faithfulness. This principle is more than avoiding fraud or fulfilling obligations; it's about embodying God's heart in all financial dealings.

CHAPTER 3:

THE PARABLE OF THE TALENTS: A LESSON IN STEWARDSHIP

Matthew 25:14-30 presents the Parable of the Talents, a story that emphasizes the importance of managing God-given resources wisely.

Let's dive into this delightful tale with an open heart to obey God with our financial situation.

Picture this: a wealthy man, prepping for a long journey, decides to entrust his vast fortune to his servants. This isn't just any handover—he's doling out hefty sums, showcasing his trust and high expectations. He hands five talents (think more like hefty gold bars) to one servant, two to another, and a single talent to the third, each according to their ability. Note the brilliance here: our man with the cash is no fool; he's divvying up the dosh based on competence.

Fast forward to the return of our traveling tycoon, eager to see what his merry band of money managers has achieved. The first servant, armed with five talents, has been busier than a bee in a lavender field.

He's doubled his stash, earning a jubilant "Bravo!" and a promotion. The second chap, with his two talents, has also been hard at work, doubling his pile and receiving similar accolades. Both are rewarded with even greater responsibilities—a clear nod to the value of industriousness and effective management.

Then, enter the third servant, stage left, with all the flair of a damp squib. Gripped by fear and a rather dismal view of his master looking down at the ground, he's done nothing more than dig a hole and hide his talent. His master's reaction? Less "well done" and more "what on earth were you thinking?"

He's promptly labeled lazy and wicked, his talent is taken away, and he's left to gnash his teeth in the outer darkness—a dramatic lesson in wasted potential.

This parable isn't just a biblical bedtime story; it's a clarion call to action.

The Parable of the Talents teaches us that stewardship isn't about what we start with, but how cleverly and courageously we use it. Success in God's kingdom hinges on taking risks, making bold moves, and multiplying what we've been given. It's a masterclass in turning potential into prosperity, showing that faith and effort are the real gold standards.

This parable vividly illustrates stewardship. Diligent management of resources gets a thumbs up, while neglect and fear lead to a proper telling off. Money, when used shrewdly and ethically, speaks well of us before God. But when misused or hoarded, it sings a different tune—one of judgment.

Matthew 20:16 nails it: "So the last shall be first, and the first last: for many are called, but few chosen."

Money is a lot like energy—it needs to flow and grow. When God blesses you, He wants you to multiply that blessing, not sit on it like a dragon on a hoard. He wants to see you expand with it and enjoy the fruits. This was God's first directive.

Genesis 1:28 says it best: "Then God blessed them, and God said to them, 'Be fruitful and multiply; fill the earth and subdue it; have dominion over the fish of the sea, over the birds of the air, and over every living thing that moves on the earth.'"

God desires for us to multiply, not just biologically. But He wants us to expand and have full dominion over our health, over our wealth, and the world we create while we are here.

Now, take a look at our old pal from the Parable of the Talents—the one who buried his talent in the ground. I've met this character a thousand times in real life. He's the one who, paralyzed by fear of failure, misses the golden opportunity to expand and prosper. Instead of stepping out in faith, he retreats, clinging to the false security of inaction.

It's like he's forgotten that God is ever-present, ready to guide us through the storms of uncertainty. This is the bloke who acts as if God isn't there to help him weather the tough times, the one who lets fear eclipse faith, and ends up squandering the potential for growth.

It doesn't matter where you are today—whether you're broke, buried in debt, or feeling the relentless pressure of unpaid taxes. You might feel trapped, as if the weight of despair is crushing your spirit. But here's the truth: God can and will turn it around if you are willing to let Him lead.

One of the things He requires of us is to be good stewards. Now, there's a lot to unpack about what being a "good steward" looks like, but before we dive into the practical to-dos and what-not-to-dos, we need to address your relationship with money. Because if we don't fix how you see money, no amount of advice on what to do will make a difference.

Let's get real—your mindset towards money needs a transformation. It's not about hoarding it in fear or spending it recklessly. It's about understanding money as a tool to fulfill God's purpose, to expand His kingdom, and to bless others.

Relevance to Your Life

Reflect on your relationship with money. Do you see it as a divine tool, entrusted by God to bless others and fulfill His purposes? Or do you treat it like a dragon hoarding gold, guarding it with jealousy?

Your financial choices speak volumes about your values and priorities, reflecting your trust in God's provision and your commitment to using His gifts wisely.

Avoid the extremes: I'm not suggesting you give away all your money or donate indiscriminately. Instead, be open to God's guidance on where your money should go.

Remember, the purpose of money is threefold:

1. To exchange value: Money isn't meant to sit idle like in some vault. It's a medium to facilitate exchange,

helping you acquire what you need while providing for others.

2. To multiply and expand: Think of money like seeds. Plant them wisely, and they'll grow. Invest in opportunities that multiply your resources, reflecting the parable of the talents. God wants you to flourish, not stagnate.

3. To give you freedom to obey God: Financial freedom isn't about buying a private island (though that does sound awesome). It's about having the liberty to follow God's calling without the chains of debt or financial worry.

Are you willing to follow His lead, or are you hiding your talents out of fear or greed? How will money speak on your behalf?

Imagine your money could talk. Would it say, "I've been used to expand God's kingdom," or would it grumble about being stashed away, growing moldy from neglect? Money, like a well-trained dog, should be obedient, ready to go where God directs.

Let's keep it real—this isn't a license for reckless spending or random acts of charity. It's about strategic generosity, where every dollar reflects your faith in God's abundance.

Are you investing in ways that align with His purposes, or are you burying your talents in the backyard, hoping no one notices or possibly just a reckless spender who doesn't have a clear path and vision from God?

Our relationship and how we view money will determine how we behave with it.

CHAPTER 4:

THE DUALITY OF MONEY'S RELATIONSHIP WITH GOD'S CHILDREN

Let's Get Rich NOW!

Ah, the siren song of getting rich quick—it's about as sensible as a screen door on a submarine. Money is the ultimate shapeshifter: a blessing in disguise or a curse in plain sight, depending on how you handle it.

Let's explore the biblical perspective on the dual nature of money.

When viewed through the lens of divine stewardship, money becomes more than just a tool. It morphs into a voice that speaks of our character, integrity, and faithfulness. By embracing this concept of money's duality, we can navigate the complexities of wealth with wisdom and grace, aligning our financial actions with God's eternal purposes.

This is a critical point, and we as God's chosen people cannot afford to let this aspect of our relationship with money slip into the unknown. We need to know where we stand with money.

Do not try to get rich by means that disrespect God. That's the definition of "getting rich quick." It doesn't mean you can't make money quickly, but it means avoiding the world's shortcuts that lead to money being your master.

Here are some Bible verses that caution against trying to get rich quickly:

1. Proverbs 13:11: "Wealth gained hastily will dwindle, but whoever gathers little by little will increase it."
2. Proverbs 28:20: "A faithful person will be richly blessed, but one eager to get rich will not go unpunished."

Its clear, don't take the shortcut, do it right.

Take it from me, someone who had to learn the hard way, there's a balance to all this stewardship stuff. Giving is good, keeping things in order is good. Having access to capital is good, expanding is good! But here's the dark side to money as well. We can't give our way to riches, we can't keep our way to wealth, and we can't hoard our way to prosperity. There's a good chance you can even expand your way to destruction. I will touch more on this through the next few chapters, but we really want to understand the broad overview of the " duality of money" to make sure we now have the right mindset to act!

The Blessing of Money:

Picture money as your loyal butler—dressed in a crisp suit, always ready to serve you a steaming cup of opportunity. When money is your servant and not your master, it becomes an incredibly powerful tool for good. It's like having a trusty sidekick in a superhero movie, always there to back you up on your grand missions, whether they're about building schools, feeding the hungry, or supporting your local cat café.

Proverbs 3:9-10 puts it beautifully: "Honor the Lord with your wealth, with the firstfruits of all your crops; then your barns will be filled to overflowing, and your vats will brim over with new wine." In other words, when you put God first and manage your wealth wisely, abundance follows. Money becomes that friend who helps you out, the one who's always got your back, enabling you to do good and make a positive impact.

The Curse of Money:

Ah, but here comes the twist—money has a dark side. Imagine this: one day, your trusty butler decides he's had enough of your orders. Suddenly, he's calling the shots, and you're the one serving him tea. When money starts to rule over you, it's like giving the villain the keys to the city. Proverbs 28:20 warns us, "A faithful person will be richly blessed, but one eager to get rich will not go unpunished." It's a stark reminder that chasing quick riches can lead you down a slippery slope from hero to zero.

When money becomes your master, it's like letting a power-hungry CEO run wild without any checks and balances. Suddenly, it's dictating your life—deciding how you dress, where you live, and even who you associate with. This shift in power can lead to pride, making choices solely to advance yourself, and hoarding wealth for personal gain. And then, before you know it, relationships crumble, debts pile up, and that once-helpful butler is now a tyrant.

Let's break this duality down further:

Blessing Money:
When you're the master, you're steering the ship. Money listens to you, and you direct it to where it can do the most good. You're building God's kingdom, investing wisely, and storing and growing your wealth responsibly. Imagine a

garden—you're planting seeds (money), watering them with faith and good stewardship, and reaping a bountiful harvest that you can share with others. This is the ideal scenario where money is a blessing, a tool that amplifies your ability to make a positive difference.

Cursing Money:
But flip the script, and money starts planting its own seeds— of greed, pride, and deceit. You're no longer in control. Instead of growing a beautiful garden, you're stuck in a dense jungle of financial woes and broken relationships, taxes and burdens. Money's curse is in its power to ensnare those who let it dominate their lives. You end up with debts that feel like quicksand, pulling you deeper the more you struggle. Relationships strain under the weight of financial stress, and the joy of giving and sharing is replaced with the anxiety of hoarding and loss.

Managing the Dual Nature of Money:
So, how do you stay in the blessing zone? Simple but not easy, Be a good steward follow God's Spirit. Recognize that money is a tool, not a deity. Treat it with respect but never let it sit on the throne of your heart. When money becomes your master, it's like letting a power-hungry CEO run wild without any checks and balances. Suddenly, it's dictating your life—deciding how you dress, where you live, and even who you associate with.

This shift in power can lead to pride, making choices solely to advance yourself, and hoarding wealth for personal gain. And then, before you know it, relationships crumble, debts pile up, and that once-helpful butler is now a tyrant. The freedom that God wanted to give you is now overtaken by the chasing of money.

There's no middle ground here. Money can overtake you, or you can rule it. No one can serve two masters.

The Blessing and the Cursing of Money
So, we've established the dual nature of money—a blessing or a curse, depending on who holds the reins. Now, let's delve deeper, uncovering the layers of this financial onion without shedding a tear (unless it's from laughter).

Now that we've tackled the rollercoaster ride of blessings and curses that come with managing money, let's strap in for the next thrilling chapter. Picture yourself as a spiritual Warren Buffett, but with fewer gray suits and more divine inspiration. We're about to explore how to build wealth the Kingdom way, with principles that will have you seeking God's kingdom first and trading in the cutthroat world of competition for a life of creative abundance.

So, grab your gardening gloves, because it's time to cultivate a life that blooms with God's blessings. Welcome to Chapter 4: Building Wealth the Kingdom Way. Ready? Let's dive in!

CHAPTER 5:
BUILDING WEALTH THE KINGDOM WAY

Alright, folks, buckle up! We're diving into the "how-tos" and the "to-dos" of building wealth the Kingdom way. No more tiptoeing around; it's time for actionable insights sprinkled with a dash of wit and a whole lot of biblical wisdom. Here are two foundational principles that will transform our approach to money and prosperity:

When it comes to the divine art of building wealth the Kingdom way, two foundational principles will transform our approach to money and prosperity. These principles are:

1.   Seek First the Kingdom of God
2.   Operate Through Creativity, Not Competition

Let's kick things off with the first principle:

Seek First the Kingdom of God

Matthew 6:33: "But seek first the kingdom of God and His righteousness, and all these things shall be added to you."

"Seek God's kingdom for your family, for your health, for your business, and for your wealth."

Imagine your wealth-building journey not as tending a garden, but as nurturing a mighty oak tree. Instead of scrambling for immediate gains like squirrels after acorns, we align ourselves with the grand blueprint of the divine arborist—God's Kingdom while building wealth on earth. This isn't about ticking a spiritual checkbox but about letting His grand design seep into every root and branch of our lives.

When our financial pursuits are rooted in Kingdom values, they stretch beyond self-centered ambitions, growing into extensions of God's work on earth. Remember Solomon's choice when handed a divine blank cheque? He didn't go for gold-plated chariots or a palace made of marble. Nope, Solomon asked for wisdom. Because he prioritized the Kingdom, God threw in wealth and honor as a bonus (1 Kings 3:5-14). Talk about a heavenly BOGO deal!

Now, let's debunk a myth: Seeking God's Kingdom first doesn't mean you need to live like a medieval monk surviving on bread and water. It's about smart stewardship. God's Kingdom is a realm of abundance, not scarcity. You can still enjoy life's luxuries—family vacations, fine dining, and showering your loved ones with gifts—while being generous and purpose-driven.

Here's a fascinating paradox: The more you align with the Kingdom, the less you fear wealth. It's as if you're letting go of the purse strings and handing them over to God, who knows exactly what to do with them. Aligning our finances with His purposes plugs us into an endless source of provision, transforming our view on prosperity from "grab all you can" to "give all you can by God's leading."

This leads us to the next principal

Operate Through Creativity, Not Competition
Proverbs 8:12: "I, wisdom, dwell with prudence, and I find knowledge and discretion."

The second foundational principle is to operate through creativity rather than competition. The world's system often sees wealth as a zero-sum game—your gain is my loss, and vice versa. This mentality fosters competition, envy, and strife. It makes me shake my head when believers talk like this in business. In God's Kingdom, wealth isn't a pie to be divided; it's a buffet where there's always room for more plates.

Competition can drive motives that don't glorify God. Remember the story of Cain and Abel? Both brought offerings to God, but only Abel's was accepted. Instead of seeking to improve his own offering by seeking God's wisdom, Cain let jealousy and competition consume him, leading to tragic consequences (Genesis 4:1-8). This tale starkly reminds us that competition, when fueled by envy, leads to destructive outcomes. This happens when we look at another person and then compare ourselves to their life versus us looking to God and our purpose here on earth.

Creativity, in contrast, is a divine attribute. God is the ultimate Creator, and being made in His image, we're endowed with the capacity to create and innovate. Operating through creativity means tapping into an endless source of ideas and solutions—not just inventing new products, but finding novel ways to solve problems and serve others.

Here's a MASSIVE "to-do" Prayer: Think of prayer as a brainstorming session with the ultimate Creative Director. It's during these moments that divine ideas often emerge, surpassing any "hack" or "nootropic" you might find on the market. God invites us to co-create with Him, transforming seemingly impossible problems into testimonies of His provision.

Biblical stories abound with examples of divine creativity. Remember the widow's oil in 2 Kings 4:1-7? Facing financial ruin and the threat of her sons being taken as slaves, she sought help from Elisha. His peculiar instruction to gather empty vessels and pour her small amount of oil into them resulted in a miraculous, overflowing abundance. It's like a divine life hack for financial ruin—Elisha's God-inspired ingenuity turned a dire situation into an opportunity for prosperity.

Or take the feeding of the five thousand (John 6:1-14). With only five loaves of bread and two fish, Jesus fed a multitude. This wasn't just a miraculous potluck; it was a testament to God's ability to provide abundantly through creative means. Jesus didn't need a grand banquet to feed the crowd; He used what was available and, through divine intervention, created more than enough. It's like the original food truck rally, but with miracles instead of menus.

Then there's Joseph (Genesis 37-50). Sold into slavery and later imprisoned, Joseph's journey was a series of unfortunate events. Yet, through God's creative guidance, he interpreted Pharaoh's dreams and devised a plan to save Egypt from famine. Joseph's rise from prisoner to prime minister (and billionaire) overnight is a masterclass in how God's creative solutions can elevate us from our lowest points to places of influence and prosperity. His story highlights the importance of trusting in God's creative wisdom, even when circumstances seem bleak.

These stories collectively underscore a profound truth: God's creativity is limitless and multifaceted. It can transform scarcity into abundance, elevate us from despair to triumph, and turn ordinary situations into extraordinary testimonies of His power. When we embrace this divine creativity in our own lives, we open ourselves to innovative solutions and unexpected blessings. By aligning with God's creative nature, we position ourselves to receive and steward His abundant provisions, turning every challenge into an opportunity for divine intervention and prosperity.

This should fill you with hope to trust in His creativity and be open to praying about situations, believing that God will give you the answer! Creativity allows us to move past the zero-sum game mentality. It's about finding new pathways and opportunities where none seemed to exist by trusting in God.

In the Kingdom economy, this creative approach is not just beneficial but essential. When we operate with a mindset of abundance and creativity, we tap into divine inspiration that leads to innovative solutions and unprecedented prosperity. This aligns perfectly with God's nature as the ultimate Creator.

Let's also remember that creativity isn't confined to inventing new products. It's about innovative problem-solving, discovering new ways to serve others, and creating value in every aspect of life. Whether you're an entrepreneur, an artist, or a homemaker, creativity can transform your work into a divine act of co-creation with God.

So, let's swap the competition for creativity, align ourselves with the divine, and watch as God's abundant provision flows into every aspect of our lives.

And remember, folks: If God can make a mighty oak out of a little acorn, imagine what He can do with your life when you seek His Kingdom first and let your creativity run wild. After all, why settle for being a branch when you can be the whole tree? Now, go forth and prosper—Kingdom style!

CHAPTER 6:
FINANCIAL FREEDOM – GOD'S WAY

Ah, freedom—it's like the sweet scent of freshly brewed coffee on a crisp morning. God is the ultimate connoisseur of freedom, and He's beckoning us to join Him in this liberating experience. He created us in His image, not just to resemble Him, but to embody His attributes. And what's one of the most powerful attributes of God? Freedom. We can find this through seeking His kingdom first and walking in co-creativity with Him.

Finances, in this world, grant us a tangible taste of that freedom. With financial freedom, we have the ability to glorify God in ways that go beyond mere survival. It's about using that freedom wisely and intentionally to advance His kingdom.

Now, let's address the elephant in the room. A lot of people are living in some of the worst financial times many of us have ever seen. Taxes, inflation, economic downturns—you name it.

But here's the kicker: the challenge isn't the economy, the recession, or the latest financial crisis. The real challenge is using our money wisely and saving every penny we can, in ways that allow us to get ahead.

Remember the biblical wisdom in storing up? There's a fine line between saving with purpose and hoarding out of fear. Proverbs 21:20 tells us, "The wise store up choice food and olive oil, but fools gulp theirs down." Storing up isn't about building a hoard of gold; it's about being prepared, being wise, and being ready to act when God calls, So you MIGHT have a hoard of gold, according to what is right in your purpose and leading by God's spirit.

So, what does this duality look like? Imagine a squirrel. Yes, a squirrel. Squirrels gather and store nuts for the winter, but they don't just stash them all in one place. They scatter their hoard, knowing that some will be lost, but enough will be there when they need it. That's us with our finances— diversified, purposeful, and guided by divine wisdom.

The Bible also warns us against the foolishness of hoarding. In Luke 12:16-21, the Parable of the Rich Fool, Jesus tells of a man who hoarded his wealth without considering his spiritual state. The moral? Wealth without purpose is vanity. It's not just about saving; it's about saving with God's purpose in mind.

Let's talk about the essence of freedom God desires for us. In Galatians 5:1, Paul writes, "It is for freedom that Christ has set us free. Stand firm, then, and do not let yourselves be burdened again by a yoke of slavery." God wants us to be free from financial stress and anxiety, enabling us to make choices that align with His will and glorify Him. He doesn't want us to walk in a state of perpetual worry, but in a state of peace and readiness to say "yes" to His calling.

When we talk about financial freedom, it's not just about the absence of debt or the abundance of wealth. It's about having the freedom to act according to God's will, to be generous, to invest wisely, and to live without the constant burden of financial strain. You may need a TON of debt to leverage the wealth you are about to build. But it would be done wisely and with God's leading.

Example: Buying a very successful company that God has opened the door to, however you don't have enough to purchase the whole thing, but you may feel Gods leading you to own this. He will provide and make sure everything is secure.

2 Corinthians 9:8 reminds us, "And God is able to bless you abundantly, so that in all things at all times, having all that you need, you will abound in every good work."

So, in these challenging financial times, the focus should be on wise stewardship. Yes, the economy is unpredictable, and inflation can feel like an uninvited guest who just won't leave, but our task is to navigate these waters with God's wisdom.

Now is the time to rise up and prosper. In these moments of economic uncertainty, we have a unique opportunity to demonstrate our trust in God and our commitment to His principles. By seeking His kingdom first, we can tap into a level of creativity and resourcefulness that goes beyond mere human ingenuity. This isn't just about surviving—it's about thriving and using our financial freedom to make a lasting impact.

When we align our financial decisions with God's will, we are not just storing up for ourselves but investing in His eternal kingdom as we follow Him and live freely. This kind of stewardship leads to true freedom—freedom from worry, freedom to give, and freedom to follow God's calling wherever it may lead. It's time to embrace this freedom, to step into our God-given role as stewards of His resources, and to use our finances to glorify Him in every possible way.

CHAPTER 7:

NOW IS THE TIME TO RISE UP AND PROSPER

Act Now, Get Ready, and Embrace Your Calling

Alright, folks, the time has come. No more waiting on the sidelines or pondering what might have been. Now is the time to act. Now is the time to get ready and align ourselves with God's Kingdom in our calling and practicality.

There are many more pieces to wealth that we can find in God's Word. Our goal should be to fervently seek the Lord for wisdom about how to direct the use of our money and ensure we follow His Kingdom principles in every aspect of our lives.

Here's the kicker: it doesn't matter where you are right now. Feeling like you're in total ruin? Today is the day to rise up and tell the Lord, "It's time for me to take on my calling." Say it out loud and let Him guide you into your future.

It's like finally deciding to follow the GPS instead of wandering aimlessly with a map that doesn't have all the roads.

Seek Wisdom from the Ultimate Source

God has a clear stance on seeking guidance. He says don't go to fortune tellers or star-readers if you want to know what's coming next. Instead, come to Him. He wouldn't make such a point about it if He wasn't open to revealing His plans to us. We just need to approach Him with the right heart. This includes our finances and how we steward them.

James 1:5 says, "If any of you lacks wisdom, you should ask God, who gives generously to all without finding fault, and it will be given to you." So, why settle for guesswork when you can get wisdom straight from the source? It's like choosing a gourmet meal prepared by a master chef over a fast-food burger.

Get Practical with Your Calling

Being a good steward isn't just about lofty ideals; it's about practical action. Proverbs 21:5 reminds us, "The plans of the diligent lead to profit as surely as haste leads to poverty." We need to make plans, set goals, and take steps forward— no matter how small they might seem.

I would like for you to pause and write down what your next financial step would be, no matter how small or big, it could be saving and saying no to spending on something that you know has been taking up your money and freedom from God, or something large like tackling a large Debt. Today is time to pray, get clear on God's vision and use those talents to bring God glory.

Remember the parable of the talents in Matthew 25:14-30? The servants who invested their talents wisely were praised and rewarded. The one who buried his out of fear was rebuked. God expects us to use and grow what He has given us, not hide it away.

Embrace the Present and Plan for the Future

It's easy to get stuck thinking about what could go wrong, but we need to shift our focus. Philippians 4:6-7 encourages us, "Do not be anxious about anything, but in every situation, by prayer and petition, with thanksgiving, present your requests to God. And the peace of God, which transcends all understanding, will guard your hearts and your minds in Christ Jesus."

Instead of worrying, let's get proactive. Whether it's getting out of debt, starting a business, or simply being more generous, the time to start is now. Not tomorrow, not next week, but today. It's like planting a tree—the best time was 20 years ago; the second-best time is now.

Trust in God's Provision

God's provision isn't just a safety net; it's a launching pad. Malachi 3:10 says, "Bring the whole tithe into the storehouse, that there may be food in my house. Test me in this," says the Lord Almighty, "and see if I will not throw open the floodgates of heaven and pour out so much blessing that there will not be room enough to store it."

This isn't just about tithing; it's about trusting that when we align with God's will and act in faith, He will provide abundantly. It's more than this, but It's kinda like investing in a stock with guaranteed returns because the CEO is infallible. However we have to make sure our heart is in the right place as well.

Take the Leap of Faith

Now is the time to take a leap of faith. Hebrews 11:1 defines faith as "confidence in what we hope for and assurance about what we do not see." It's time to stop worrying about the "what ifs" and start embracing the "what can be."

So here's the plan: Step out, seek God's wisdom, act with diligence, and trust in His provision. Remember, you're not just planting seeds for tomorrow; you're building a legacy of faith and stewardship that will echo into eternity.

And if you ever doubt, just think of Peter walking on water. Sure, he sank a bit, but he also did something miraculous simply by stepping out of the boat. So, what are you waiting for? Get out of the boat and start walking on the water of God's promises. Because now is the time, and you've got a divine appointment to keep.

CHAPTER 8:

FINDING YOUR PURPOSE IN CHRIST

Alright, folks, here we are—the grand finale, the pièce de résistance. We're diving into finding your purpose in Christ. This isn't just a vague sense of direction; it's about discovering that laser-focused, God-given mission that gets you up in the morning with a spring in your step. And trust me, it's a journey packed with enough wisdom, laughter, and divine nudges to keep you entertained and enlightened.

First things first: let's get one thing straight. Just because you desire to do what's right doesn't necessarily mean you're going to do what's right. Romans 7:15 hits home: "I do not understand what I do. For what I want to do I do not do, but what I hate I do." It's a bit like deciding to eat healthily and then finding yourself elbow-deep in a bag of chips. Desiring to follow God's path is just the start; we need a clear vision and a whole lot of seeking the Lord.

Seek the Lord and Hear from God

Proverbs 3:5-6 gives us a roadmap: "Trust in the Lord with all your heart and lean not on your own understanding; in all your ways submit to him, and he will make your paths straight." I used to think this ment, just sit there and wait for God's understanding to come, later I found out that it was more about finding God's leading as I was moving forward in everything I do. In other words, don't try to wing it. Instead, lean into God's wisdom, which often comes through prayer, scripture, and those quiet moments when you're not distracted by the latest Netflix series. Ps... I don't have netflix, it's a distraction from God's calling in your life for $16.97 per month.

Jeremiah 29:11 is another gem: "For I know the plans I have for you, declares the Lord, plans to prosper you and not to harm you, plans to give you hope and a future." God's got the blueprints for your life, and they're way better than anything you could draft up on your own. So why not go straight to the source?

Matthew 6:33 lays it out: "But seek first the kingdom of God and His righteousness, and all these things shall be added to you." This is where things get exciting. When you prioritize God's Kingdom, everything else falls into place like a perfectly solved Rubik's Cube. Suddenly, life's complexities start to make sense, and you find that sweet spot where purpose, creativity, and provision meet.

Philippians 4:19 assures us: "And my God will meet all your needs according to the riches of his glory in Christ Jesus." It's like having a divine ATM card with unlimited access to God's blessings. You seek Him first, and He takes care of the rest. Simple, right? Well, it takes faith, prayer, Discipline, wisdom, and persistence, but the payoff is worth it.

Refinement and Testing

Now, here's the part where it gets real. God doesn't just hand you your purpose on a silver platter. Sometimes, He refines you through tests and trials. James 1:2-4 says it best: "Consider it pure joy, my brothers and sisters, whenever you face trials of many kinds, because you know that the testing of your faith produces perseverance. Let perseverance finish its work so that you may be mature and complete, not lacking anything."

Think of it as a spiritual boot camp. Just like muscles grow through resistance, your faith and character are strengthened through challenges. It's all part of God's master plan to shape you into the best version of yourself.

1 Peter 1:6-7 adds, "In all this you greatly rejoice, though now for a little while you may have had to suffer grief in all kinds of trials. These have come so that the proven genuineness of your faith—of greater worth than gold—may result in praise, glory, and honor when Jesus Christ is revealed."

The Joy of Purpose

Finding your purpose in Christ isn't just about enduring tests; it's also about experiencing the joy and fulfillment that comes with living out God's plan for your life. Psalm 37:4 encourages us: "Take delight in the Lord, and he will give you the desires of your heart." As you align your desires with God's will, you'll find a deep sense of satisfaction and joy that transcends any earthly pleasure.

A Call to Action

So, where do you go from here? It's time to take action. Ephesians 2:10 reminds us: "For we are God's handiwork, created in Christ Jesus to do good works, which God prepared in advance for us to do."

Proverbs 16:3 provides the final piece of the puzzle: "Commit to the Lord whatever you do, and he will establish your plans." It's a partnership—your commitment and God's establishment. Together, you're unstoppable.

CLOSING THOUGHTS

As we wrap up this journey, remember that finding your purpose in Christ is a lifelong adventure filled with discovery, growth, and a lot of divine guidance. It's not always easy, but it's always worth it.

So, dear reader, go forth with confidence. Seek the Lord with all your heart, lean into His wisdom, embrace the refining process, and delight in the journey. You've got a divine purpose that's uniquely yours, and there's no better time than now to start living it out.

If you enjoyed this book so far, I would love it if you could follow me on Instagram @Jlouishardy for more insights and updates. Also, your feedback means a lot to me! Please consider leaving a review on Amazon to share your thoughts and help others discover the book. Your support is greatly appreciated and helps spread the message further. Thank you!

May God bless you, With Health, Wealth, and Influence.

https://

mudssmmaclogin.my.site.com/providerPortal/login ?

Made in the USA
Monee, IL
22 September 2024

66246768R00036